DATE DUE

618.92
GLA   Glaser, Jason.

              Chicken pox

First Facts™

Health Matters

Chicken Pox

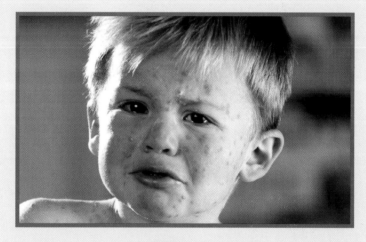

by Jason Glaser

Consultant:
James R. Hubbard, MD
Fellow in the American Academy of Pediatrics
Iowa Medical Society
West Des Moines, Iowa

Capstone
press

Mankato, Minnesota

First Facts is published by Capstone Press,
151 Good Counsel Drive, P.O. Box 669, Mankato, Minnesota 56002.
www.capstonepress.com

Library of Congress Cataloging-in-Publication Data
Glaser, Jason.
    Chicken pox / by Jason Glaser.
    p. cm.—(First facts. Health matters)
    Includes bibliographical references and index.
    ISBN 0-7368-4288-8 (hardcover)
1. Chickenpox—Juvenile literature. I. Title. II. Series.
RJ406.C45G56 2006
618.92'914—dc22   2004028549

Summary: Introduces readers to chicken pox and its symptoms, treatments, and prevention.

Editorial Credits
Mari C. Schuh, editor; Juliette Peters, designer; Kelly Garvin, photo researcher/photo editor

Photo Credits
BananaStock Ltd., 18–19
Brand X Pictures, 1
Capstone Press/Karon Dubke, cover (foreground), 8, 9, 14, 15, 16 (background), 21
Corbis/Jose Luis Pelaez Inc., 13; Lester B. Bergman, 16 (inset)
Image Source/elektraVision, 6–7
Photo Researchers Inc./Science Photo Library Inc./Dr. P. Marazzi, 5, (inset), 20;
    VEM, cover (background)
Visuals Unlimited/Bill Beatty, 11; Science VU, 5 (background)

1 2 3 4 5 6. 10 09 08 07 06 05

Table of Contents

What Is Chicken Pox?

Chicken pox is an illness with skin **rashes**. It is caused by a **virus**. A virus is a germ that copies itself in your body. Viruses move through your blood. The chicken pox virus moves out to the skin. Spots and **blisters** form.

Fact!
Animals do not get chicken pox. Only people get chicken pox.

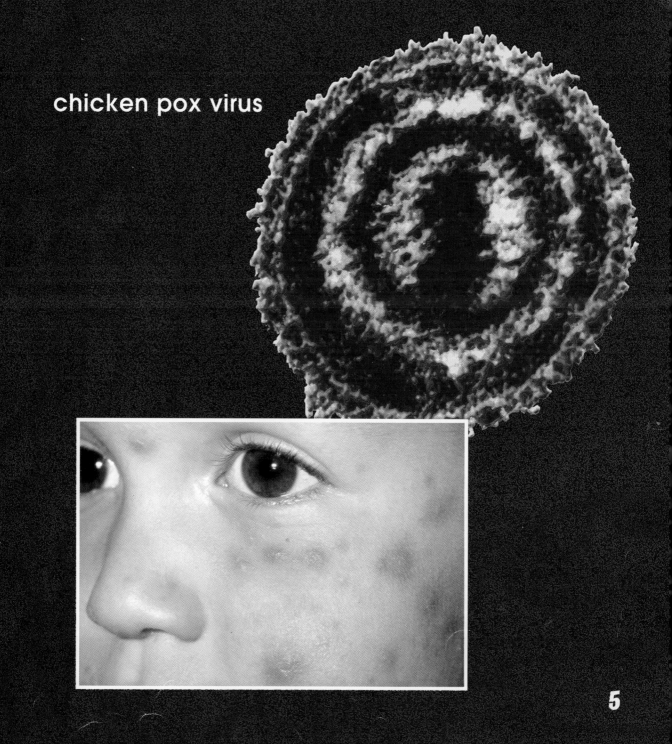

chicken pox virus

5

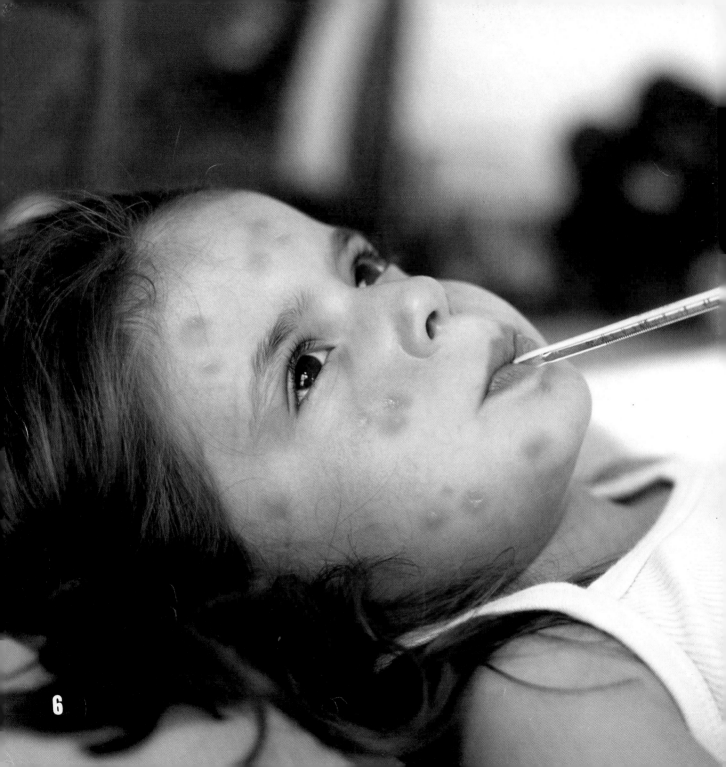

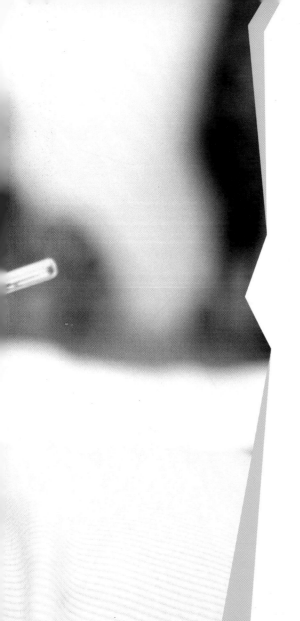

Signs of Chicken Pox

The first sign of chicken pox is itchy red spots. These spots become blisters. Blisters turn into scabs. Chicken pox has other signs. People may get a fever or a sore throat. They may also be tired. Many people don't want to eat.

Fact!
Most people get chicken pox only once.

How Do Kids Get It?

Kids can give others chicken pox before they show signs. They can sneeze or cough the virus into the air. Other kids may breathe in the virus.

Kids can get the virus by touching
chicken pox blisters. The virus gets on
their hands. It gets into their body
when they touch their nose or mouth.

What Else Could It Be?

Kids get rashes and skin problems in other ways. Measles can cause blisters and fever. Touching a plant called poison ivy can cause a bumpy rash. Some people with skin **allergies** also get rashes.

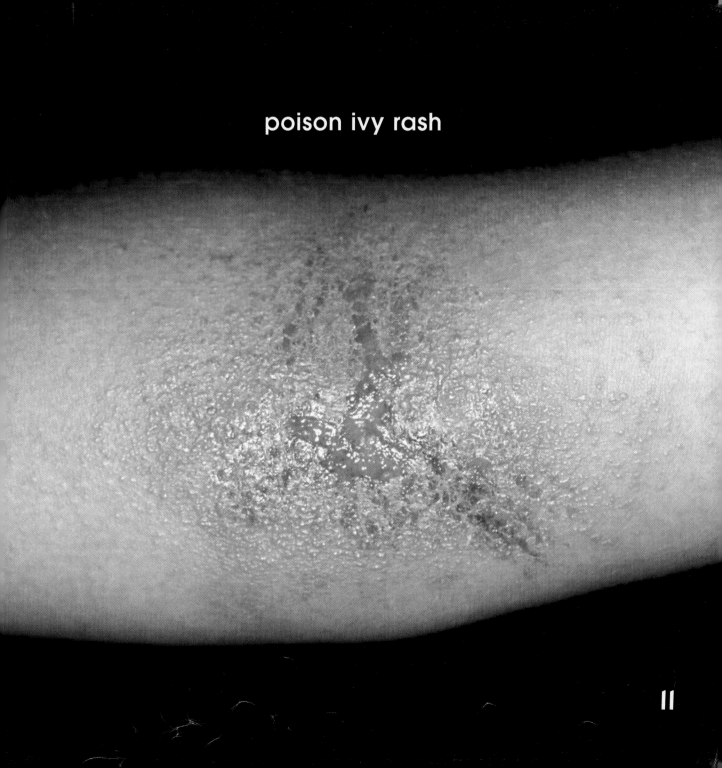

poison ivy rash

11

Should Kids See a Doctor?

Kids do not usually need to see a doctor for chicken pox. Chicken pox can be cared for at home. Going to the hospital can give the virus to other people. Bad pain and breathing problems are reasons to see a doctor.

! Fact!
Chicken pox will go away in one or two weeks.

13

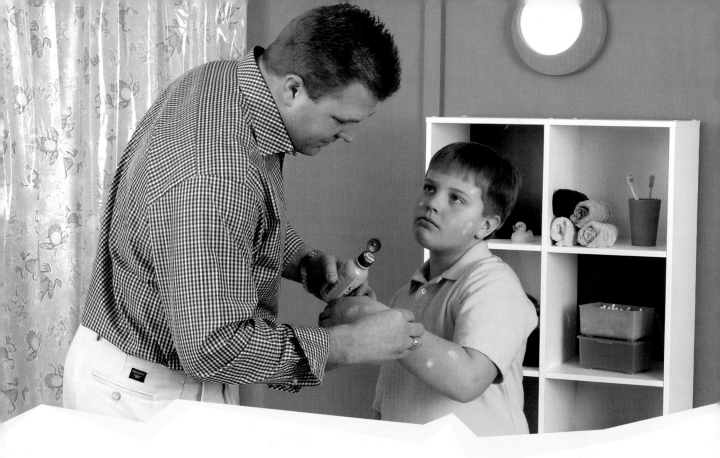

Treatment

Blisters are itchy. Kids should try not to scratch them. Bathing in warm water and baking soda can help. Adults can also put **calamine lotion** on kids' skin.

Adults can give kids safe pain **medicine.** They should follow a doctor's advice for using any medicine.

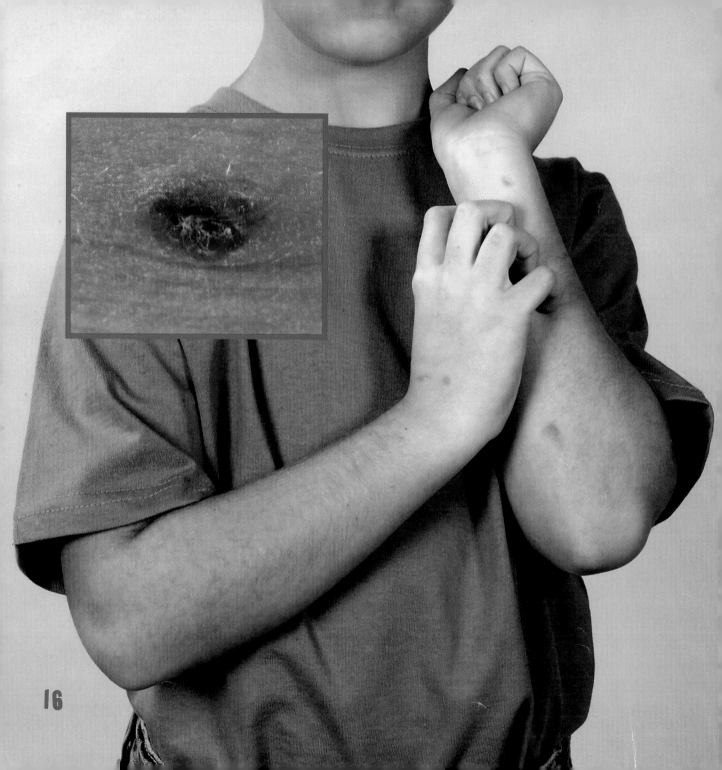

If It Gets Worse

Scratching blisters can cause problems. Germs can get into open blisters. The germs can cause **infections**.

Problems from chicken pox are worse for older kids and adults. Chicken pox can cause breathing problems and skin infections for them.

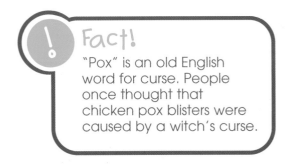

Fact!

"Pox" is an old English word for curse. People once thought that chicken pox blisters were caused by a witch's curse.

Staying Healthy

People can take steps so they don't get chicken pox. They can get a shot to prevent it. This shot will keep most people from catching the virus. Staying away from people with chicken pox can also stop it from spreading.

Fact!

In 1995, there were 4 million cases of chicken pox. Then, the chicken pox shot was created. There are now less than 800,000 cases a year.

Amazing but True!

Most children with chicken pox will get 250 to 500 blisters. Catching chicken pox from a brother or sister can cause more blisters. A brother or sister could get up to 5,000 blisters.

Brothers and sisters spend a lot of time together. At its worst stage, chicken pox can cause more blisters. Brothers and sisters often catch it during the worst stage.

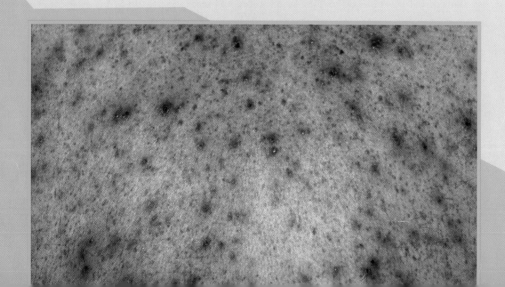

Hands On: Anti-Itch Cloth

Oatmeal is one of the oldest treatments for chicken pox itching. Have an adult help you make an oatmeal cloth to treat itchy skin.

What You Need

1 cup (240 mL) of plain instant oatmeal
blender
handkerchief
rubber band
bowl of water

What You Do

1. Use the blender to grind the oatmeal into a fine powder.
2. Spread out the handkerchief on a table. Pour the oatmeal dust onto the middle of the handkerchief.
3. Lift up the sides and corners of the handkerchief.
4. Tightly twist the handkerchief just above the top of the pile.
5. Wrap the rubber band around the twist several times to hold it closed.
6. Hold the filled part of the handkerchief in the bowl for one minute. Take it out of the water. Squeeze out the extra water.
7. Gently rub the wet part of the handkerchief on your skin.

Glossary

allergies (AL-er-jees)—reactions to things like dogs, cats, and dust

blister (BLISS-tur)—a sore bubble of skin that is filled with liquid

calamine lotion (KAL-eh-mine LOW-shen)—a lotion that dries blisters and makes skin rashes like chicken pox feel better

infection (in-FEK-shuhn)—an illness caused by germs or viruses

medicine (MED-uh-suhn)—pills or syrup that can make people feel better during an illness

rash (RASH)—an area of skin that becomes red, itchy, or irritated

virus (VY-russ)—a germ that copies itself inside the body's cells

Read More

Plum, Jennifer. *Everything You Need to Know about Chicken Pox and Shingles.* The Need to Know Library. New York: Rosen, 2001.

Royston, Angela. *Chicken Pox.* It's Catching. Chicago: Heinemann, 2002.

Silverstein, Alvin, Virginia Silverstein, and Laura Silverstein Nunn. *Chicken Pox.* My Health. New York: Franklin Watts, 2001.

Internet Sites

FactHound offers a safe, fun way to find Internet sites related to this book. All of the sites on FactHound have been researched by our staff.

Here's how:
1. Visit *www.facthound.com*
2. Type in this special code **0736842888** for age-appropriate sites. Or enter a search word related to this book for a more general search.
3. Click on the **Fetch It** button.

FactHound will fetch the best sites for you!

Index